Eating

Written by Jo Windsor

The bear likes to eat fish.

fish

The bird likes
to eat fish.

fish

The crocodile likes
to eat fish.

fish

The jellyfish likes
to eat fish.

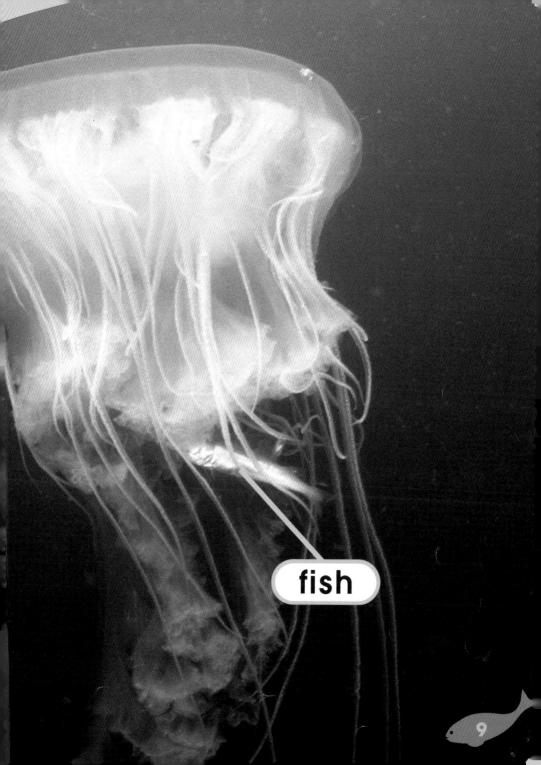

fish

9

The spider likes
to eat fish.

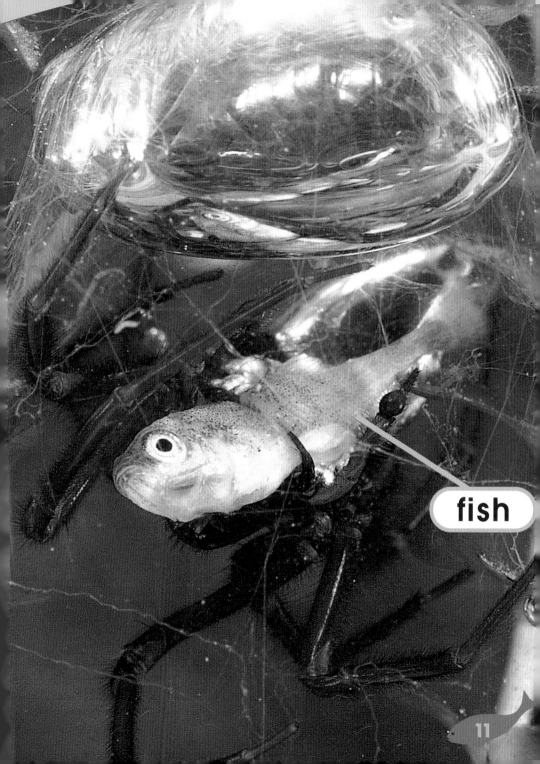

fish

The boy likes
to eat fish, too!

Index

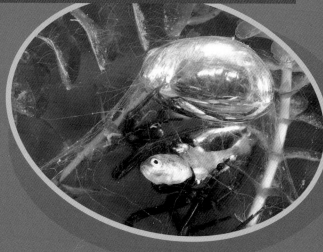

Guide Notes

Title: Eating Fish

Stage: Emergent – Magenta

Genre: Nonfiction (Expository)

Approach: Guided Reading

Processes: Thinking Critically, Exploring Language, Processing Information

Written and Visual Focus: Photographs (static images), Index, Labels

Word Count: 37

FORMING THE FOUNDATION

Tell the children that this book is mostly about eating fish.
Talk to them about what is on the front cover. Read the title and the author.
Focus the children's attention on the index and talk about the boy and the animals that are in this book.
"Walk" through the book, focusing on the photographs and talk about how the boy and the animals are eating fish.

Read the text together.

THINKING CRITICALLY

(sample questions)

After the reading
- How does the bear get the fish to eat?
- What does the bird have that helps it get the fish?

EXPLORING LANGUAGE

(ideas for selection)

Terminology
Title, cover, author, photographs

Vocabulary
Interest words: bear, fish, bird, crocodile, jellyfish, spider
High-frequency words: likes, the, to, too